# THE PSYCHOLOGICAL IMPACT OF AMERICA'S SERIAL KILLERS

# THE PSYCHOLOGICAL IMPACT OF AMERICA'S SERIAL KILLERS

## WARREN GEIS

# CONTENTS


**1** Introduction to Serial Killers 1

**2** Psychological Theories on Serial Killers 5

**3** Case Studies of Notorious American Serial Killers 9

**4** The Media's Portrayal of Serial Killers 15

**5** The Victims of Serial Killers 19

**6** Law Enforcement and Serial Killer Investigations 23

**7** Treatment and Rehabilitation of Serial Killers 27

**8** The Cultural Legacy of American Serial Killers 31

**9** Conclusion and Future Directions 35

# CHAPTER 1

# Introduction to Serial Killers

In America, serial killers are a growing breed. News story after news story seems to be dedicated to uncovering another serial killer's crimes and the outrageous atrocities they have committed. Serial killers are those who take the lives of multiple people in a systematic pattern of killings and murders. Most of the time, a serial killer has an MO, or "modus operandi," which is a preferred way of completing their crime. The MO typically shows the psychological impact a serial killer has on their victims, the same as a "hunting ground," or location where the killer will operate. Many murder detectives can tell if a certain type of killing has been done by a serial killer by checking out these patterns they create. The percentage of serial killers in the U.S. is said to be about 1% of all murders each year. Clearly, while there are quite a few of them, it's not a good idea to be judging everyone you walk by on the streets.

Serial killers have been around forever. They have a very distinct psychological impact as well as a historical one. They exist all around the world today, but their existence can be found in some of the most ancient possible history. The concept of a serial killer is descended from early human history when early man used to migrate in search of food. These early humans would begin to lose family members while traveling or lose family and migrate to a new location. Invasions and wars have also brought about declining populations. The changes in populations would allow serial killers and their practices to go undetected for long periods of time.

*Defining Serial Killers*

A person who murders three or more people is known as a serial killer. They kill two or more victims at different times, and often the nature of the criminal act differs from one to the next, according to the Federal Bureau of Investigation (FBI).

Three elements of the nature of killing differentiate serial killers: two or more individuals are affected; a "cooling off" period rests among murders, which allows the killer to return to a more regular pattern of conduct; and the killings are mostly done due to sadistic or psychotic objectives, rather than substance-based robbery.

Characterized by a range of behaviors often communicated through unusual or excessive practice, serial killers—or as speculative criminology often tags them, 'violent pilgrims'—produce a place of "fear and confusion" that outlives the growth of crimes. Violence is employed to accomplish these aims, and not extremely differing from organized crime or the rustic malevolence of 'angry trades,' in many ways this form of fear-mongering represents a power succession.

Remaining, producing material for benchmark and mass media that communicate unforgettable pictures of atrocity, many see this as a kind of dialogue or communication that is also called "Killions"—the hope is very often to hurt. Serial killers, in their plan to reveal their hatred by damaging society and every person in it as a whole, represent the most radical instance of this fear-mongering individual. They perform various acts of evil and entail the search of our understanding and the infamy of the eager mass media and an extra 7th sociology—the group responsible influences are almost merely an afterthought.

*Historical Overview*

The changes in policing, evidence gathering, and interrogation procedures in the early 1900s became a catalyst that allowed society to transform into a new frontier of unprecedented killing sprees. The progression to serial killing was fairly consistent. During the industrial revolution or at least the mid-1800s, human anatomy was just starting to make strides into medical research. One prime example is the body snatchers that benefited by selling bodies to researchers for scientific purposes. It was this era of anatomy that doctors made claims they could determine one's character by examining the bumps and shapes of the head. As the medical field advanced and joined forces with psychology, Germany in particularly sowed the seeds of psychological profiling.

Towards the close of the 1800s, the idea of an individual being insane and unable to control their murderous tendencies was being discussed in England. The final push came when psychiatrists (Alienists) testified in a Kansas criminal case and succeeded in defending a Norwegian criminal. This launched the American public into a serial killer craze, which was compounded by the high visibility given to a number of well-publicized cases. In addition to H.H. Holmes and Jack the Ripper, there was William Westervelt, a man who killed only to get rid of dental students who made sexual advances. He was followed by T.J. Gibbs, who "was fascinated by blood" and after each of his five killings he "would paint wonderful flowers in the crimson violence."

# CHAPTER 2

# Psychological Theories on Serial Killers

America has been the home or association of some of the most chilling, fascinating, and unsettling killers, many of whom have had societies more intrigued by their personalities than their crimes. Many of these murderers have developed their macabre persona through direct childhood trauma or other psychological abnormalities. Four different theories that study the psychological actions of the serial killer are relevant to the issue: 1) the prospect that a lot of serial killers fit the distinctive contentions of either psychopathy or sociopathy; 2) the argument that nature and biology have a direct link to violent behaviour; 3) the notion that serial murder can develop from early psychological abnormalities; 4) the notion that serial killers have often developed as a consequence of a loveless or singly concerned upbringing.

First comes 'evil,' which is a hypothetical, spiritual term that states that some people simply have an inherently bad nature. This concept is mostly outdated, even if it does not exclude a God or higher power, and though serial murders may be evil in the act of trying to kill, spirits have free will. The idea of psychopath or sociopath is akin to that of evil, and is invalidated by modern science.

Psychopathy and sociopathy are often compared and contrasted, and it is uncertain whether the two are fundamentally distinct personalities. Psychopaths, however, are often born, emerging at an even younger age, and are less likely to feel guilt. Furthermore, they are frequently far more cunning and manipulative than sociopaths. This has made it a more exciting concept for describing the mental activities of the serial killer, seeing as how serial murder is often premeditated and carefully planned.

### Psychopathy and Sociopathy

Psychopathy and sociopathy are psychological conditions that are very closely associated with the activity of serial killers in America and around the world. The former is a complete lack of empathy towards other human beings, as well as manipulation and deceit, which is why this group has an extremely high propensity towards violent crime.

There are a few aspects of this that are fairly uniform whenever they are discussed among psychologists and psychiatrists. First of all, the major emotional traits of psychopathy include a great deal of paranoia in their relationships, a real effort to avoid any kind of responsibility, and only the feeblest and most brief exhibition of any sort of affection. Further, psychopaths do not care about people in general, aside from how they can manipulate them to their particular ends. Of course, by now, anyone should be able to see how psychopathy is the work both of a murderer and a criminal, both organized and disorganized. Murderers simply take psychopathy to the extreme. Finally, normal people need one primary factor if they are to mourn someone: closeness. A psychopath can put on the sham of being close, can mimic all of the conventions, but in reality, the person simply is not and cannot get close to anyone because of this deadly flaw.

*Nature vs. Nurture Debate*

The debate of nature versus nurture is nested in psychology's most basic elements as the origin of behavior. This debate has stirred up many controversies through time as people decide where the fault lies for bad behavior. This is no exception when it comes to serial killers. This is not a new idea to have when looking at criminal behavior. With the rise in determining the cause of serial killing, there is a need to know if it is biologically or environmentally uncovered.

Nurture has to do with the environment and the childhood the child has had. It can also mean the emotions one might feel about his or her own surroundings. This includes the parenting he or she might have received; for example, is the mother shopping out of the Sears catalog or in the army-navy store or is the child black or white. Those basic things can either be taken for granted and it allows us to make better predictions for final outcome on things such as personality traits and behavior. With all the debate and argument of the day, there is little to no question in everyone's mind today that "all of these influences play a part in a child's development". Sanford Bates notes that "part of the difficulty we have in understanding influences become clearer".

# Case Studies of Notorious American Serial Killers

To help illustrate the psychological and social impacts of serial killers, case studies of some of the most notorious serial killers in America will be presented in this paper. Specifically, the lives, crimes, and psychological profiles are presented for three serial killers: (A) Ted Bundy, a good-looking, intelligent, and charming man who was well-educated and considered himself above his victims; (B) John Wayne Gacy, a member of the Jaycees and was involved with politics; and (C) Aileen Wuornos, a Volusia County beach girl who was adopted and from an unstable family. These three cases were chosen based on the degree of fame the case and the killer received, the bizarre nature of the crimes, and the psychological composition of the killer.

Theodore Robert Bundy was an American serial killer, kidnapper, rapist, burglar, and necrophile. He decapitated at least 12 victims and kept their heads as trophies in his apartment. He was executed in the electric chair on January 24, 1989, at Florida State Prison.

John Wayne Gacy was an American serial killer and sex offender. He was known as the Killer Clown because of the contradictory roles he would engage in. He killed 33 teenage boys and young men and buried 29 of them under his house and garage. On May 10, 1994, he was executed in the electric chair.

Aileen Carol Wuornos was a female American serial killer. She killed seven men between 1989 and 1990, claiming that they raped or assaulted her while she was working in the streets as a prostitute. She was sentenced to death and executed in 2002.

*Ted Bundy*

Theodore Bundy, also known as Ted Bundy, is one of the most widely known, but often misunderstood, notorious American serial killers. "Confession of a Killer: The Ted Bundy Tapes," directed by Joe Berlinger, describes Bundy as an attractive, talented, and successful man - a law school graduate and budding politician who was later found guilty of the murder of thirty women. With Berlinger's documentary in mind, this paper breaks down Bundy's character and the way in which he was perceived by others.

Despite showing a pattern of aggression, Ted Bundy was generally seen as an attractive and ambitious young man by his friends and acquaintances. He was a law student at the University of Puget Sound, a planned intern at Seattle Law Office, Vice President of the Seattle Law Council, and an election campaign driver for the Republican Party. He appeared intelligent, successful, polite, and well-liked by many. Carolyn Marez, a mother at the Planned Parenthood Clinic in Seattle, was recorded as thinking he was handsome, kind, and that it had been a good appointment with him. She described him as being fashionable and very outgoing with his clients, constantly chatting and laughing. His long-time girlfriend, Margot Rey, called him "the all-American kid." His neighbor, Mr. Chuck Klopp, had known Bundy for sixteen years and speaks fondly of him to the press. None of these people could have foreseen Bundy's arrest or that he was capable of mass murder. As the documentary reveals, Bundy generally attracted a good deal of positive attention. Mary-lynne Chino said, "They all thought of Ted as being really great. No one would have called Ted a criminal. Ted was everybody's dream, I'm sure. You know, nice, good-looking, popular, and totally likable. Ted was everything you'd hope for in a love child."

### John Wayne Gacy

John Wayne Gacy was born in Chicago, Illinois, on the 17th of March, 1942. He spent his childhood years living in the United States of America before young John and his family moved to West Virginia in 1949. Reports describing Gacy's time spent living with an abusive alcoholic father are littered with a plethora of his father's brutal assaults aimed not only towards John, but the rest of his family as well. Some diagnosed Gacy's father with bipolar disorder. Perhaps, this period in Gacy's life, watching his father violently abuse his mother – and the rest of the family, played a contributory role towards the making of the monster John Wayne Gacy was to some day become.

Clearly, prison was never going to teach this lifelong offender his lessons for he was a repeat offender throughout the majority of his young life. In fact, out of the twelve criminal cases and guilty pleas Gacy had within his lifetime, ten of them were handed over by the time he was just 18 years old. He's even described as "dope-pusher, get-well quick artist, thief, and sexual deviant." So, with all this in mind, it seems somewhat difficult to spot a clear and concise turning point in his life that made him become the monster he later grew to become. Overall, Gacy appeared to be driven by overwhelming "internal stressors" over the eruption of "perversion." He was also verbally abusive about the victims brutalized and murdered during the interviews he completed while alive.

### Aileen Wuornos

Widely known as the first American female serial killer, Aileen Carroll Wuornos was born in Rochester, Michigan in 1956. Lisa Kester, who is a doctoral candidate at Seton Hall University, points out that as Aileen aged, her father began being accused of crimes pertaining to pedophilia and later committed suicide. Wuornos was also raped by various men and her mother abandoned her. By the age of 11, Aileen began prostituting herself. Aileen and her grandmother clashed often, leading to her being kicked out of their home. The teenager dropped out of school at 15 and was pregnant by the age of 14. After being sexually abused by her grandfather, Wuornos gave birth and was sued by her father's parents. Kester alludes to Aileen eventually terminating her daughter's paternal rights and putting the 6-year-old child up for adoption.

Dr. Gregg O. McCrary, a former special agent of the FBI, offers another side to Aileen Wuornos in that her maternal grandparents seemed to genuinely want the child to live with them. Wuornos showed signs of extreme intelligence from an early age and was a successful high-school student compared to most youth who have gone through sexual trauma. McCrary goes on to say that Wuornos was compared to two scholarly students in the sixth grade, even scoring an impressive IQ of 143. While this intelligence, sarcasm, and general "big" personality attracted others, the deep pain of Wuornos' experiences also showed through. According to the 1998 book, Monster: My True Story by Aileen Wuornos as told to Christopher Berry-Dee, Aileen said at various times in her life that she would like to shoot down the men who abused her and the men who patronized her body. Indeed, Aileen did mature into an individual with a deeply disturbed psyche who killed at least seven men and was later sentenced to death. Wuornos was also posthumously diagnosed with BPD.

# CHAPTER 4

# The Media's Portrayal of Serial Killers

The majority of the time, the media does not show remorse when discussing serial killers and their heinous actions. Much of the time, the media takes a serial killer's face and makes them into a celebrity, which imposes a stigma as well as a potential deterioration in the public's ability to be shocked or revolted by murders. As a result, the media has an impact on our viewpoint of these kinds of ill-fated events. Films and internet shows also frequently generate revenue for news networks. People who were not born at the time of the criminal act have the chance to experience it. Print media, in turn, frequently put the killers' names in bigger letters on the front page of the paper. People are drawn to the powerful characters in literature, so the print media rewards this notion. Because the general public did not have access to serial killer specifics, many killers in the early 20th century went unrecorded.

One possible explanation for the phenomenon of the public's embrace of violence for amusement is the idea of "criminal identification." This is the concept behind the film about the "unlikely" serial killer, the one that does not quite fit one's typical snap impression of what a serial killer should be. True crime tales that go "towards confirming the viewer's existing moral outlook on the world" from a lawful point of view can be pleasurable, or entertaining in a criminal way. It is pleasurable and soothing to be literate of the particulars of our negative passions, but that one shares the killer's deviant perspectives and habits is not true. The terms "verisimilar" or "lawful" refer to the portrayal of significances of aggression in serial murders. As well as this, serial murder is merely classified as the exposé of tremendous cruelty. It is a concrete instance of barratry, dealing, or foul play. The viewer must surmise that the killers are blanketed by something customized to portray relatable main characters.

*True Crime Culture*

What is true crime? Serial killers and sadistic criminals have fascinated and disturbed the world for centuries, and America is no exception. America has produced the most well-known serial killers to date, including Ted Bundy, Jeffrey Dahmer, John Wayne Gacy, and Aileen Wournos, as well as numerous prolific killers documented in the critically praised TV show Mindhunter. The existence of true crime shows and websites indicates that "true crime" is the factual recounting of a specific crime, including the investigation, the trial, and the demographics of the criminal. News reporting on any criminal activity, on the other hand, can be classified as true crime, or is often called as such by victim advocacy and anti-violence groups for the purpose of crime awareness and prevention. The genre of true crime has a broad appeal and fan base, the overall focus of which is a harsher approach and requirements that use any and all personal and private material to castigate or praise the actions of the protagonists.

True crime reflects an era of low social trust, as the ability to commit such ruthless acts of violence with little discord requires severe pathological detachment. A sickness of the human mind allows, if exploited, the criminals to be romanticized by truth seekers with a proclivity for the macabre. The lengthy investigation of these heinous crimes, and the sad detail of the criminal investigation, while troubling to most, rejuvenates the blood thirst of the public. As a result, the media funds and submits more true crime content to eager fans and the cycle continues. Even so, the murder and sexual assault of women and children has long been used for public enjoyment. Nevertheless, the non-radical movements and binary-terminist views of contemporary feminism significantly influence the form of that state social perspective.

*Impact on Public Perception*

The portrayal of serial killers in the media isn't just about what it shows, but also, and perhaps more importantly, what it isn't showing. A cursory glance at the long list of serial killers in America, of all flavors, appearances, and motivations, shows us a collection of marginalized, alienated, and isolated people. And this only makes sense: for a person to commit such brutal acts, there would be a need to distance themselves from anyone who cares about them, and who would care if they made the news.

Since 1989, when Jeffrey Dahmer was arrested, there have been only 50 truly solo serial killers in America. The majority of active serial killers were a team, almost entirely family members with a partner or a few non-family members, as is consistent with historical statistics about serial killing, where there is a negligible number of true solo actors. And there's nothing more alienating than being an extremist, either to the left or right, given that, for example, at last count, there have been 302 separated, specialized extremist groups in the United States. And to be clear, they all claim to be solo actors; but in the complete list of groups in America, this is extremely rare. For all the media talk of "lone wolves," the actual animals are few and far between.

Looking at the American town and neighborhood photos, one looks for the hell that the "lone wolves" leave as they pass through: massive homicides, torture, Nazi extremism, extreme family-size negligence, hoarding, and abuse. And when having a discussion about Ted Bundy, a cheerleader who killed 33 women after practicing on his auto his whole life while remembering practicing on a few animals, this is what needed to be addressed. When discussing what it would mean to have robbed so many, the unspoken horrors they leave when passing through, both in the living and the dead, that path was not taken.

In short, the larger question is this: How does the unhealed, the pathos, affect the surrounding community? How can you recognize and see the unhealed? Typically, NBC shows us.

# CHAPTER 5

# The Victims of Serial Killers

The mental and psychological impact is not the sole territory of the killer. A new field of research, "victimology," focuses on how people are associated with notorious criminals, their lifestyles, and how being around a suspect or known killer affects societal reputation. The people who accompany killers, after the fact, are not necessarily deemed safe themselves. Friends and family suffer the brunt of psychological abuse from a notorious and extremely hated killer. This long-term event is not usually discussed in-depth for the friends and family of accused killers.

Furthermore, some families of the victims of serial killers are left in the dark when the killer of their loved one goes unsolved. The not-knowing gives a different kind of mental pain over the years. Confession of the murder alone is not enough to satisfy the mourning loved one unless a violent killer is taken off the streets and from society completely. Serial killers do not only affect society and the families of the victims but also the serial killer's friends and families. In the documentary "The Jeffrey Dahmer Files," one of Dahmer's neighbors claims the skull of a victim hung above her bedroom without her knowledge of who Dahmer really was. The people who know him seemed to have felt under obligation to explain his actions to the documentary producers. Because of this, extensive guilt seems to lie on their conscience. Their friends are seen in the documentary nervous and depressed as they describe what living near Jeffrey Dahmer did to them.

*Understanding Victimology*

The term victimology stems from the relationship of the victim and the offender. In connection with the increased interest in violent crime over the past few decades, the number of serial killer cases has become more recognized and studied by researchers of the criminal justice and psychology fields. Prior to the 1990s, the public had no idea what the term serial killer actually meant and the various types of individuals involved within this analysis of violent criminal behavior. Offenders who torture and kill multiple victims over an extended period can wreak havoc over a large region, nationwide, and three to four multiple countries in today's glocalized society. J. Levi Martin (2005) states that media "begs to focus on the perpetrators of violence, detaching the individual from the setting in which their crime occurred" and not representing the victims.

The media drew further attention as serial killing was made more like a made-for-TV movie than a real-life drama. The United States quickly dedicated federal, state, and local law enforcement agencies to begin educating the public regarding the characteristics of the serial killer, a person who comes in a variety of personalities and kills on average three to eight victims. After the year of the serial killer, three hypotheses were drawn. Some empirical studies have supported these hypotheses, while others have failed. After three hypotheses were drawn, people did not know how to react and alert the public to actions the public could take to protect themselves from becoming a victim. Many times, the public does not know how to protect themselves from the next crime.

*Long-term Effects on Families*

Long-term victims are understandably angry at much of the popular culture focus on the killer, but studies of the long-term impact on the families of victims and the children of the killer have been few. A psychological understanding of the effects on the families was the subject of a study from the UK on the families who made the decision to go along to trial to see a young son. Another study with a similar purpose interviewed the family of an infamous British child murderer sixteen years after the defendant's execution.

While the families of long-term victims are at risk of anxiety, guilt, and anger, the feelings on the families when the killer is a son have apparently never been studied. One researcher is quoted as saying, "We, as a society, have a hard time even thinking about it. We might argue over who is the luckier, but we can find another job, see another friend. There is no fairy tale ending. It follows people for generations." The children of killers carry both a stigmatized and feared identity: they are bad - their father was a killer. A National Society for Prevention of Cruelty to Children document cites a case study of the widow, "I have to hide the truth from my two boys. It will destroy them. Everyone here knows what my husband did, but nobody discusses it. He was a monster. My sons are not. They deserve the best."

# CHAPTER 6

# Law Enforcement and Serial Killer Investigations

The formal definition of a serial killer is a person who has killed three or more persons in at least three separate incidents with a cooling off period (the time pursuing other interests between murders) between each murder. A serial killer is an individual who follows no generalized homicidal method, but instead is compelled to kill much more powerfully than the average individual thanks to deep-seated psychological and emotional disturbances. Since law enforcement does not often come into contact with the true motives of serial killers (in particular first responders), the service's understanding of serial killers is somewhat less comprehensive. The task of the criminal psychologist, also termed a "profiler," is to get inside the head of the killer and understand the motives. Of course, those motives cannot be brought back into alignment with social norms, but understanding why a killer killed as they did is vital for the investigation.

It is conjectured that serial killings have ancient origins, but the phenomenon of serial killing emerged in the US mostly during the 1970s. In addition, the number of recorded cases in the US accounts for almost one third of all known historical cases since 1520. More recent works dealing with the characteristics of serial killings predominantly come from the US, a nation that prides itself on producing the majority of the world's greatest scientists. Investigative advances and technology have allowed the narrowing down of suspects in the present day and age; however, some cold cases continue to remain unexplainable and unresolved, often adding to the enigma and mythology surrounding specific characters of interest.

### Profiling Techniques

While exact numbers are hard to come by, there is little doubt that throughout history, there were and are still today at least several hundred active serial killers. According to the FBI, by definition, a serial killer is any person who has murdered three or more people over a period of more than a month, with downtime (a "cooling off" period) between the murders. Serial killers are a rare phenomenon. As a consequence, law enforcement agencies initially applied traditional psychological profiling techniques based on case studies and expert interviews. Other profiling techniques include eye-tracking-based search tasks, functional magnetic resonance imaging (fMRI) - brain imaging, polymerase chain reaction (PCR) - testing from genetic markers, and psychopathy neural nets and automation. The nature and psychology of serial killer activity is complex and vast. Hence, this chapter presents a detailed description of classical psychological profiling techniques.

Broadly, the psychological profiling techniques address the following issues: Autobiography, Home Setting, Selection of Victims, Offense Location, Modus Operandi (MO) and Signature or Calling Card, Control, Use of Violence, Corpses, Pictures and Trophies, Sexual Activity, Exit and Escape. In particular, the "home setting" aspect refers to the possibility of multiple unreported crimes in one locale. It also explores the impact on serial killers for a change from their usual terrain. Serial murder is almost always a metropolitan occurrence. Part of the reason is the rapidly declining geographical distances necessary for travel. A concise psychological model of serial killer activity aids in the profiling work as well by signposting specific psychological differences. First, a cross-sectional look is taken at "typical" serial killers: traits, lifestyles, convictions, approaches, body-dumping site choices, and lives. Then a motivational ladder is identified, representing from initial motive through to later stages of escalation and violence.

### Cold Cases

More recently, this approach is failing and has given rise to the "murder script," where the crime itself serves as a scripted form of macabre performance art with the intention of achieving fame and, in some idealistic listeners, emulators. Some of the notoriety sought is intended to be post mortem (i.e., achieved through a spectacular "showdown" with law enforcement or committing a "non-childish" act of violence such as suicide or cop-killer homicides). But, the desire to be known and recognized has never been more apparent as in the actions of our serial killers today. Both unsolved and solved cases can become "cold." A cold case simply implies that new information has warranted further investigation, or we have a lag in the investigative process (it has accumulated into a stack of papers, exhibits, and audiotape—which speaks nothing, lest it is brought to life by a good detective). Often, impossible suspects must be cleared until the pure suspect is found—often ex post facto. Psychological clearance of a suspect is often the vital step in defrosting the old case.

The prototypical model of the serial killer "on a spree," as we discussed above, is but one. Analyzing that a body count of less than three is more likely not to be solved or is solved to the victim's benefit, often at the investigative detriment, is more often the rule than the exception. It is also apparent, with a few noted futile exceptions, that once a predilection for murder is noted, clues and even confessions beg authorities to investigate a laundry list of "cold cases" through the serial "mind-lensed" filter. Such "dusted-off" cases are often called "the answer to everything" or "the end of the rainbow" and are most often unsolved. Their presence is felt by every detective, who must deal with the 'unknown' in every corner of part I. True cold cases are the unsolved cases of the un-thoroughly investigated suspect whose MO has yoked the case with another victim-vacant individual. Very few "real" serial killers get caught but those that do often enjoy practical freedom by virtue of their reduced motion, the assurance of no future victims, and the knowledge of their every move monitored. The retired FBI agent Ressler would say "it is merely a waiting game now" and another expert/veteran about the modern-day killers is heard to confide to a prosecutor, "I don't think I can press charges until I solve ten other unsolved ones."

# CHAPTER 7

# Treatment and Rehabilitation of Serial Killers

The idea of treating serial killers is tantalizing, with recent evidence indicating that as many as half of them begin their murderous career as a result of ongoing antisocial activities, substance abuse, and aggression. From a purely humanitarian perspective, one would want to direct treatment towards those on the spectrum who are unable to contain their criminal behavior (and ultimately to protect society) and to those who have already been detected and incarcerated. The ethical considerations of mandatory treatment interventions are mostly problematic, however, and many argue that the involuntary commitment to a mental ward of a facility and the possible mandatory medical interventions could ultimately be worse than the crime itself.

Do treatments or methods for rehabilitating violent individuals work? One response is that treatments are irrelevant if the only option presented to judges and mental health professionals is to detain for the public's safety. From a correctional perspective, the treatment of violent individuals or the rehabilitation cannot be seen as effective if the person is detained indefinitely. Moreover, any rehabilitation and treatment will be surrounded by an ethical and legal swamp since their victims are frequently marginalized and bereft of any influential organizations or individuals in the political process to protect their own interests. The impact that adult, adolescent, and juvenile males with a diagnosis of severe antisocial activities have on society at large is anathema to a successful treatment philosophy. Cases that involve individuals who commit unspeakable crimes such as a serial killer or anyone who has killed innocent victims will remain too emotional and controversial for a logical or rational compromise.

*Ethical Considerations*

Many factors could contribute to the fascination with some serial killers, as Tusing and Maier have outlined. Regardless, notoriety puts a burden on our society that may be difficult to meet. Given the impact that notoriety has on the legal system, notoriety must be acknowledged and redirected when possible by the investigative and interrogatory professionals. The attention that serial killers attract can be generally characterized by the moral and psychological views that people have when dealing with their caprices. When delivered, the death penalty was irrevocable and often very far removed from the event to which it purported to deliver a response. Whether or not a moral imperative to heal, to save, or to understand can be said to exist, the unwavering view propounded here is that individuals raised in certain locations and in certain conditions are in need of psychological attention, diagnosis, and remediation. However, this view does raise conflicts especially in the light of some societies' penal policies and the nature of the psychological diagnosis and explanation which have ethical and philosophical implications of their own.

A therapeutic approach to such individuals is incompatible with current Western attitudes towards punishment, law enforcement, and penal values. Alongside this, psychological theorizing is by and large ignored within the judicial arena. Yet worse still, engaging with the quirks and conceits of disturbed individuals may offer little to those dealing with such miscreants in practical settings. Guiding ethical principles in direct managing of these peoples is the pursuit of the well-being of the patient, and this includes confidentiality, beneficence, and autonomy/independent decisional capacity. The high public interest in these individuals shapes the way in which we should proceed and, when offering treatment, address the inclusion of various other ethical principles, such as distributive justice, veracity, and justice. It is also noteworthy how the media has globalized the debates that are discussed here. Legal systems also offer protection for various individuals, but in the United States, Roberts v. United States Jaycees claimed a constitutional right to autonomy which the state legislatures could not override. This could potentially supersede confidentiality guidelines in order to ensure public safety.

*Effectiveness of Interventions*

The rehabilitation of serial killers One question remaining to be addressed is why certain people become serial killers and what, if anything, might be done to stop them. Note that this question is specifically referring to phenomena such as copies or desperate imitators of their alleged heroes. Focus here will be on the ethical issue of treating killers, as there may, after the commission of a crime, be fundamentally two aims for interventions to take place. One is the ameliorative task of providing a certain individual at risk of becoming one himself with an alternative aiming - that is, healthier - outlook on his life, his own self, and whatever victim or victims he might be brewing in his operating system.

The other is the protective task of intervening so as to prevent a predisposed person from implementing violence. Such interventions do not necessarily follow up on behavior after such behavior has been commenced. Psychoanalysis might be interesting from an individual standpoint because it is able to approach motor patterns of conduct from desire first rather than from aversion; Freud is able to ask in a fundamental way why the person does nothing when his sight-blocking tendencies are confronted with a dead body in a pool of blood. The group seminar approach, even if relatively more anonymous, may also be effective. A direct and, to an equal measure, restrained approach to receivers may be most effective. Yet, is this actually so? It is a well-known fact that we are not especially good at discovering psychopaths by pure clinical testing.

# CHAPTER 8

# The Cultural Legacy of American Serial Killers

Part 1: The Cultural Legacy of American Serial Killers The "Hollywoodization" of American serial killers shapes a domestic and international stereotype grounded in pop culture. The serial murderer is often white, male, and middle-class. Many killers since Dahmer and Bundy copy decades of depictions. Yet the macabre glamour of the serial murderer entwines with profound American cultural recognition of the unusual mental state. European Gothic was born of an ambivalent love-loathing for ordinary folk who become extraordinary in their loss of common humanity. Gothic lives on in the dark cul-de-sacs behind suburban picket fences as a serial killer, who aesthetically restores the loss of individual sameness. The renewed emphasis of FBI agents on solving cold cases, particularly those associated with serial killers, reveals both the general cultural fascination with the subject as well as the issue of the hundreds of thousands of Americans who are missing and can never be forgotten.

Part 2: The Impact inside the Circle Members and objects within the social networks initially affected by serial murder are also deeply affected by the psychological pressure the investigation exerts on their routines. Certainly, the magpie journalist befriends and shoulders the fears of victims so the title of journalist includes aspects of the construction of the trauma narrative – the heroes of their own stories. Journalists write of how life in fear changes an individual's tastes, particularly the experience of architectural changes. Although there is no standard way to react to trauma, the recuperative impact of the cultivation of memorialization is easily traced in the vast amount of profiles. Psychiatrist Thomas Bond ranks the post-trauma impact of the 19th-century Ripper murders at a five due to the positive changes the world experienced through the final creation of the field of forensic science. Other researchers believe that the doctrines of human rights transformed for the better as a result of the muckraking done by journalists covering the American Red Scare.

*Influence on Pop Culture*

America has given rise to some of the most notorious serial killers in history. Names such as Ted Bundy, Jeffrey Dahmer, and John Wayne Gacy immediately come to mind. Few could imagine that men like these are to be seen as inspirations for a book plot or that female groupies would send them love letters and ask to bear their children. We refuse to be disgusted and repulsed by these individuals, who had no regard for human life and inflicted unbearable suffering upon their victims.

Like pseudo-events, serial killers have infiltrated our society so deeply that they will never escape us, death and all. We are fascinated by them. They have become such a part of American culture that they are seen as famous; they are seen as stars in a sense. In a way, this is how American culture mesmerizes us and continues to haunt the notion of resisting corruption.

The folklore of America is inundated with true stories of murder and madness, but the serial killer has left an indelible mark on our lives and entertainment spectacles. The psychopathic and antisocial behavior of these criminals has had a significant effect on popular culture. Serial killers such as Ted Bundy, John Wayne Gacy, and even Jeffrey Dahmer have gained a following of fans, and films are based on their doings. Our fascination with evil has yielded a string of blockbuster films. Because of our morbid wish to stare into the face of the Medusa, screenwriters and movie directors have managed to create an award-winning filmography dedicated to the executioner's deadly urge and the lawman's relentless attempts to capture him. Messages are glamorized for the silver screen.

### Memorialization of Victims

Ritualistic funeral practices date back as far as the Upper-Paleolithic era, and in modern culture, we still utilize traditional practices to memorialize the dead. Ritualistic violence is also included in these practices. In murders with a ritualistic motivation, the victim is usually a stranger who is chosen specifically for their death, and the act is considered functional because it advances the killer's tenets and practices. Religion could be the motivator behind these actions or death with a purpose of 'sending a message' or 'righting a wrong'. People, and especially Americans have been using this type of serial killer violence as a way to address ongoing concerns for many years. Many experts feel responsibility and ways to get involved in a situation by use of memorials.

Societal memorialization can incorporate emotional identification of victims and responsibility fears. Victims are memorialized as a way of reassuring oneself that they acted in a "responsibly appropriate manner." They are also used as a substitute to understanding the true logic of the crimes. Individual level engagement and motivation factors involve those who lack personal skills to solicit such movement, targeted layoffs and having a victim (or street) as one's 'personal it' which results in excessive attachments to the incident. Early registration in a memorandum of some sort is also a factor, and increases with repetition of the attack within an area.

# CHAPTER 9

# Conclusion and Future Directions

This essay has sought to elucidate the psychological impact of America's serial killers. A number of features that are deemed to be common to many serial killers have been identified, and while the presence of these alone does not make someone a killer, it is of interest to consider what factors might be at play to enable these individuals to lead parallel lives that are sufficiently non-dissonant so that the killers tend to be able to live lives that appear outwardly to be fairly ordinary. Furthermore, the observation that in some cases, the psychological disturbance that the killer displays is relatively minor and can lead to the conclusion that a number of serial killers know full well the consequences of their actions and are prepared to disregard these to participate in murders that they view as both fun and exciting.

In the real world, these changes have an enormous bearing on the victims and their families. Increased awareness of the phenomenon, therefore, should have a number of implications for mental health services, given that being a close relative of a serial killer can lead to feelings of shame, stigma, and revulsion, with individuals' mental and physical health also suffering. There may also be a case to consider what level of threat such children pose to their contemporaries, given the fact that the emergence of what Blaming & DeLisi call 'youthful killers' has been, at least in part, tied to acquaintance with older homicidal role models. Subjecting children with such disturbed backgrounds and propensities to strenuous intervention from an early age might well serve to stabilize their behavior and be in the potential victims' interest. Finally, given that typical future serial killers often leave a trail of dead animals behind them, Children's Services staff should be alert to both signs of overt abuse and also the psychodynamics between the child and their pet that can reveal abuse.

### Implications for Mental Health Services

Although the vast majority of people with mental health problems are not going to become serial killers, mental health services still have a responsibility for addressing any possible consequences of the activities of serial killers or potential effects on the public. It may be important, therefore, for the field of mental health services to consider what some of these consequences might be, particularly if they are either occurring or likely to arise as a result of the impact of serial killers. This section considers what the implications might be for mental health services.

Some might argue that the field of mental health services has had involvement with providing information about psychopathic and sexual murderers to the public, since individual clinicians have appeared at training workshops for the police and the public. Again, this is rarely the case, however. Finally, some might argue that works are being produced by those in the field of mental health exploring a variety of topics from psychopathic murderers and people who are repulsed by blood to documentary films about murder. Although these types of books and articles are expository, however, and rarely retail in excessive detail murders or explicit and gory material, some express great concerns about the way in which they may shape public attitudes. All the issues to do with public computing, the crimes of the individual and the social and historical role of the serial killer are important questions for the field of mental health that require further research.

*Preventative Measures*

In the majority of published liaison interpretations of serial murder, only potential directions for dealing with its more immediately visible societal pathologies are discussed. Most of this treatment is inordinately pessimistic. We are left with a sense of the serial killer's eventual imbrication in the very social body whose diseases we wish to heal. We know "a great deal about man's predatory acts and their contributors, but we know very little about how to initiate fuel therapeutically satisfying solutions to these problems on a collective rather than individual basis." Once we "get past the moratorium of horror that such a series of violations of the current moral order provokes in the Press and among the public, the first uneven steps will bring about several exotic outcomes." Suggestions of this nature, often enough, are merely analogues of the kill. It is babysitting pure and simple?

Worse, then, would it not be virtually possible or plausible to change the psychic, social, and moral consequences of the very existence and/or acts of serial killers? It seems to me that it might. The obverse would negate anything etiolative, any psycho-physiological investigation of antecedents. I need scarcely stress here the need for utilization and extension of the sort of therapeutic (and preventative) techniques utilized by the Swiss Training School for Police. Psycho-somnambular technicians, in conjunction with psychiatrists and laypeople, are working out increasingly infallible stratagems for

allowing the patient to come into the closest possible praxis inter-re-
lationship with his fantasied reality... with a wife, say, or a child-vic-
tim. Teleology comes full circle; the 'causal' symbiosis of background
and outcome a one-to-one harmony. And so serial murder stops, and
with it the horror of the deracination.